DOG

Jill Foran and
Katie Gillespie

PETS WE LOVE

AV2

www.av2books.com

Step 1
Go to **www.av2books.com**

Step 2
Enter this unique code

XLPDW1XZO

Step 3
Explore your interactive eBook!

CONTENTS

AV2 is optimized for use on any device

Your interactive eBook comes with...

Contents
Browse a live contents page to easily navigate through resources

Audio
Listen to sections of the book read aloud

Videos
Watch informative video clips

Weblinks
Gain additional information for research

Try This!
Complete activities and hands-on experiments

Key Words
Study vocabulary, and complete a matching word activity

Quizzes
Test your knowledge

Slideshows
View images and captions

... and much, much more!

PETS WE LOVE
DOG

Contents

Puppy Pals

People all over the world keep dogs as pets. Dogs are intelligent, faithful, and extremely loving animals. A dog can comfort you when you are feeling sad or lonely. She can also be trained to perform important jobs. There are special guide dogs, police dogs, and herding dogs. For many reasons, adding a dog to your family can be a rewarding experience.

However, despite their positive qualities, it is not easy to own a dog. They require a lot of time and commitment. Dogs must be fed, groomed, played with, and cared for on a daily basis. If you are willing to be patient, the love that you receive from your dog will make the effort of caring for her worthwhile.

Owners should groom their dogs regularly. A complete grooming routine includes bathing, brushing, nail trimming, and ear and teeth cleaning.

There are about **90 million** pet dogs in the United States.

More than **3 million** dogs end up in U.S. shelters every year.

The United States has more than **10,000** pet stores.

There are more than **340** dog breeds around the world.

Miacis developed into a dog-like animal called **Cynodictis** about 30 to 40 million years ago.

Dogs may have been **domesticated** between 20,000 and 40,000 years ago.

There were at least five types of **dogs** in existence in **4,500** BC.

Wolves are dogs' closest nondomestic relatives. Both belong to the genus *Canis*. A genus is a group of animals or plants that have common characteristics.

From Wild to Mild

Dogs have lived on Earth for many years. The majority of scientists agree that all species of dogs, including wolves, foxes, coyotes, and domestic dogs, **evolved** from the same creature. This animal was a weasel-like, tree-climbing mammal known as *Miacis*.

Out of all the animals in the world, dogs have been associated with people the longest. It is believed that thousands of years ago, dogs visited human villages to look for discarded food. In exchange for guarding livestock, assisting with hunting, and warning of danger, people offered dogs food and shelter.

Soon, humans discovered how useful dogs could be. They grew to depend on dogs, both for protection and for companionship. Over time, dogs began to be bred to meet specific needs.

Today, many dogs are trained to assist people with disabilities. Guide dogs help visually impaired people.

Pet Profile

There are many different dog breeds to choose from. You must learn more about the ones that interest you before buying a new pet. Dog breeds are grouped according to their roles, behavior, and features. Each breed has certain characteristics that make it unique. Think about the dog features that are most important to you and your family.

Golden Retrievers
- Belong to the **sporting group**
- Are one of the world's most popular household dogs
- Have a dense **coat** that repels water
- Are very friendly and eager to please
- Respected for their tracking abilities
- Are a patient breed

Basenjis
- Belong to the **hound group**
- Are **tricolor**, chestnut red, or black in color
- Have a short, smooth coat
- Are an extremely affectionate breed
- Were once used as hunting dogs in Africa
- Are very patient
- Enjoy being independent

Chinese Shar-Peis
- Belong to the **non-sporting group**
- Have a rough coat and wrinkled skin
- Are one of the oldest recognized breeds, dating back more than 2,200 years
- Have an average life span of 7 to 10 years
- Prefer the company of humans
- Were once used as fighting dogs in China
- Have a large head

Border Collies
- Belong to the **herding group**
- Are usually black in color
- Have white markings
- Are very energetic and intelligent
- Considered the best sheep-herding dog on Earth
- Are eager to please

Siberian Huskies
- Belong to the **working group**
- Can have brown or blue eyes, or even one of each color
- Are very friendly
- Have a gentle temperament
- Require a lot of exercise
- Are used to pull sleds in certain cold climates

Chihuahuas
- Belong to the **toy group**
- Have a dome-shaped skull
- Are the smallest dog breed
- Have a long, smooth coat
- Do not like cold weather
- Can be aggressive
- Are curious and alert

Miniature pinschers are native to Germany. The breed became popular in the United States in the 1920s.

Chihuahuas usually weigh no more than **6 pounds.** **(2.7 kilograms)**

Labradors are the **most popular dog breed** in the United States.

Great Danes can be up to **32 inches** tall at the shoulder. **(81 centimeters)**

Picking Your Pet

Getting a dog is a big commitment. There are many things to consider before you add a furry friend to your family. Since there are so many different breeds, you should research which types of dog are the best fit for you.

How Much Will My Dog Cost?
Having a dog can be very expensive. However, there are different options available to fit a variety of budgets and lifestyles. You can buy your dog from a breeder or a pet store. This can be costly, but may be worth the price. **Purebred** dogs are typically the most expensive. Alternatively, you may want to rescue your dog from an animal shelter. This will cost much less, and give an animal in need a loving home. You should factor in the cost of food, **veterinary** care, and other supplies your dog will need as well. These costs are ongoing throughout your dog's lifetime.

What Do I Have Time For?
Puppies are cute, but they require a lot more care and attention than an adult dog. It is important to be realistic about the amount of time and energy you have to spend with your dog. Certain breeds may need extra time for training. Long-haired dogs **shed** more than short-haired dogs. They also require additional grooming. Make sure you choose a dog that you will be able to care for properly.

Life Cycle

As your pet grows older, he will have different requirements. You should know what your dog needs at each stage in his development. No matter how old your dog is, he must be given lots of love and affection.

Newborn Puppy

Newborn puppies are almost totally helpless when they are born. They cannot walk, and are both deaf and blind. Newborn puppies spend plenty of time drinking their mothers' milk. They also sleep for long periods. It is important for newborn puppies to be kept warm.

Maturity

Adult dogs can be healthy for many years. They will live long, happy lives if they are well-cared for. However, older dogs do slow down eventually. Many start to lose their eyesight and hearing. Your dog may need extra care and attention as he gets older.

Three to Nine Weeks

At three weeks old, puppies are able to see, hear, and walk. By four weeks of age, they are ready to begin exploring. They are ready to be weaned when their teeth start to grow. This occurs sometime between four and seven weeks. At nine weeks, they are ready to eat puppy food. Puppies must stay with their mother and **littermates** until they are at least eight weeks old.

One Year

At one year, most puppies are full grown. However, some dogs will continue to gain weight until age two. Dogs at this stage of development have learned many things. Their mental skills are fully developed. It is important for one-year-old dogs to get plenty of playtime and exercise.

Puppies experience the world by chewing. Chewable toys will help them learn good behavior and keep them from chewing other items in the house.

Dog Supplies

To ensure a smooth transition for your new dog, stock up on the essential supplies ahead of time. You will need many important things, including food and water dishes, a leash and collar, a brush, a bed, and toys.

It is necessary to own a leash for your dog so that you can take her for walks. By wearing a leash, your dog will be safe from speeding cars and other outdoor dangers. Not only is a leash important for your dog's safety, it also helps with training. Use your dog's leash to teach her to heel, sit, and walk nicely.

Another item you must have for your new pet is a dog bed. They come in many different shapes, sizes, and styles. Above all, it should be soft and warm to make your dog feel comfortable.

Place your dog's bed in a quiet area of her own to keep her happy. You can even put a hot-water bottle in her bed if she is nervous. This will remind her of the warmth of her mother and littermates, and help to calm her down.

When choosing toys for your dog, make sure you select ones that are an appropriate strength and size. Toys that are too weak or too small may be accidentally swallowed. This can be very dangerous for your pet.

In the United States, the Food and Drug Administration (FDA) regulates food for dogs and other pets. The FDA ensures that pet food is safe to eat and that pet food labels have the correct information.

Dog Diets

There are many different kinds and brands of dog food. It may be dry, in the form of kibble. Dog food can also be wet and stored in a can. There are even special formulas available for young puppies and senior dogs.

You can buy dog food from a veterinary clinic, pet store, or grocery store. To make sure that you are feeding your dog the right type of food, talk to your veterinarian. She will know which brands are best suited to your breed of dog.

It is also important to find out how much you should feed your dog, and how often. Your veterinarian will advise you on the correct amount to feed your dog at all stages of his development.

Young dogs need more frequent meals than older dogs. It is a good idea to feed your dog at the same times every day. Always make sure your dog has a dish full of fresh water to drink.

When your dog is training or exhibiting good behavior, you can feed him treats. Dog biscuits are a good choice because they help keep your dog's teeth healthy. Be careful not to give your dog too many treats. They may lack the nutrients your dog needs. It is essential to feed your dog a balanced diet.

From Nose to Toes

Dogs come in a wide variety of shapes, sizes, and colors. Ranging from the tiny Chihuahua to the gigantic Irish wolfhound, many dog breeds look quite different from one another. However, despite these differences, all dogs share the same **ancestors**. For this reason, all dogs have a number of similar physical features.

Teeth

Dogs have very sharp canine teeth that are used to hold **prey**. Their molars are good for grinding food.

Tail

A dog uses her tail to communicate emotions. A tucked in tail indicates fear, while a wagging tail may show that she is happy or excited.

Ears

Dogs have a keen sense of hearing. This is because their ears are excellent sound receivers and locators.

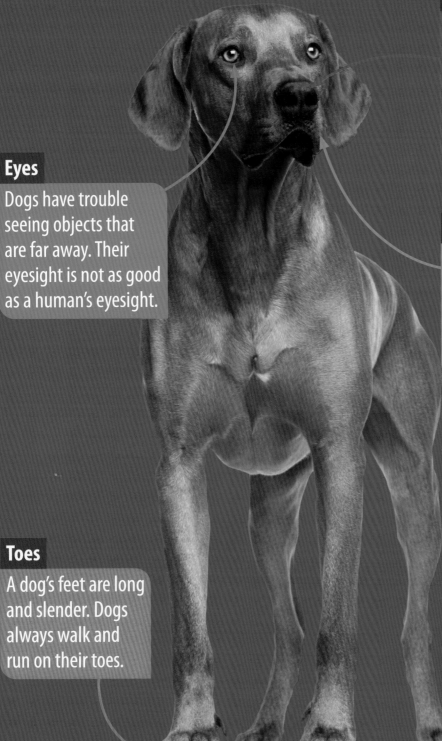

Nose

A dog's nose is extremely sensitive. She uses it to smell and identify things, and to control her body temperature.

Eyes

Dogs have trouble seeing objects that are far away. Their eyesight is not as good as a human's eyesight.

Whiskers

A dog has whiskers on her chin, **muzzle**, and cheeks. She uses them to touch and feel her surroundings.

Paws

Dogs have tough pads on the bottoms of their paws. These pads are used to absorb shock.

Toes

A dog's feet are long and slender. Dogs always walk and run on their toes.

Dogs can develop ear infections if their ears get wet. To prevent this, owners should avoid pouring water directly on the dog's head during baths.

Great Grooming

Keeping your dog clean is a major responsibility. You must groom your dog's ears, paws, and coat regularly. This will ensure that he is looking and feeling his best. Depending on his breed, your dog will require a particular amount of grooming. Short-haired dogs need less attention than long-haired dogs.

Always brush your dog's fur in the same direction that it grows. Start with his back, then hold his head up to brush down his throat. Next, brush between his front legs. Be very careful when brushing your dog's stomach. The hairs here are fine, and his skin is more sensitive, so it is important to be gentle.

Grooming your dog's coat will help remove dirt. Regular brushing also massages your dog's skin, and promotes circulation. It is important to brush your dog often to help keep him clean.

Most dogs do not need to be bathed very often. If their coats are well-maintained, and they spend the majority of their time indoors, they should only require three or four baths a year. When bathing your dog, use a shampoo designed for dogs or puppies. This will be gentler than a regular shampoo. Also, make sure to restrain your dog so he does not struggle and hurt himself.

Dogs should be taken to the veterinarian for a check-up once a year.

There are about 113,300 **veterinarians** in the United States.

In 2018, Americans spent **$18.1 billion** on **veterinary care** for their pets.

There are **four core vaccines** for dogs.

Healthy and Happy

In general, dogs are fairly healthy animals. However, there are steps you can take to ensure your dog stays in top condition. Proper grooming and feeding will help keep your dog healthy. Check your dog every day to see if she has split toenails, ticks, or fleas.

Your dog also needs plenty of exercise. Playing with her and taking her for daily walks will help your dog stay in good shape. It is necessary for your dog to maintain a proper weight. Dogs who do not get enough exercise may become overweight. They are also at a higher risk to develop heart disease.

When you first get your dog, you should bring her to a veterinarian. He will examine your dog and let you know if any **vaccinations** should be given. In most countries, the law states that your dog must be vaccinated each year. These shots protect your dog against **rabies** and other dog diseases. Regular checkups are also an important part of maintaining your dog's health.

Agility training helps dogs form a strong bond with their owners. In agility competitions, owners direct their dogs through an obstacle course that needs to be completed within a time limit.

Dog Duties

Dogs are incredibly social animals. Years ago, when they lived in the wilderness, dogs were part of groups called packs. Every dog pack had a leader to make the rules. The leader was also responsible for watching over the other group members.

Today, most dogs think of their human family as their pack. It is important to show your dog who is the leader early on. Otherwise, he will become confused. Your dog may even try to take on the role of leader himself. You, or someone in your household, must take charge of the family pack.

Dogs are extremely intelligent. They can be trained to do many things. It is essential to teach your dog how to behave properly around other animals, especially other dogs. The best way to do this is to familiarize your dog with other animals. Let him meet new dogs so that he becomes comfortable around them. This will also make your dog a better walking companion.

Some common commands you should teach your dog include "sit," "stay," "down," "heel," and "come." It is best to start training your dog while he is still a puppy. Puppies are trained more easily than adult dogs. To help train your dog, you can take special classes at an obedience school. There are also many books available on the subject.

Harley the dog starred in the 2018 Disney movie *Patrick*. The movie's screenwriter, Vanessa Davies, and her pug, Patrick, received the Palm Dogmanitarian Award at the Cannes Film Festival.

Role Call

Dogs have appeared in countless books, commercials, television shows, and films. The first movie to star a dog was made in England in 1905. It was called *Rescued by Rover*.

One of the most famous dog characters is a collie named Lassie. She first appeared in the book *Lassie Come Home*. Written in 1940, the story is about a dog who is sold to new owners. She has to move from Yorkshire, England all the way to Scotland. Lassie's adventures start when she tries to make the long journey back home. The character has also been featured on television and in films.

Many dogs are trained to carry out important jobs in society. Guard dogs protect private homes and businesses from intruders. Herding dogs help farmers look after livestock. Dogs can even be taught to help people who are in wheelchairs.

Police and fire dogs learn how to protect people and find illegal items, such as explosives. Some breeds, such as Newfoundland dogs, are used as lifeguards on beaches. Rescue dogs can locate drowning victims. They can also sniff out survivors of earthquakes, avalanches, or other disasters.

Pet Puzzlers

What do you know about dogs? If you can answer the following questions correctly, you may be ready to own a dog.

1 Where can you buy dog food?

2 Where are miniature pinschers originally from?

3 What does a dog use its tail for?

4 From which prehistoric animal did wolves, foxes, coyotes, and domestic dogs evolve?

5 How many dog breeds are there around the world?

6 What does the FDA do to regulate pet food?

7 Which dog breed group do border collies belong to?

8 How often should a dog be vaccinated?

9 What does a complete grooming routine include?

10 When was the book *Lassie Come Home* written?

Dog Tags

Before you buy your pet dog, brainstorm some dog names you like. Some names may work better for a female dog. Others may suit a male dog. Here are just a few suggestions.

Rover

Charlie

Spot

Molly

Lucy

Sam

Jake

Benji

Max

Key Words

ancestors: early animals from which later species developed

coat: a dog's fur

evolved: developed gradually over time

herding group: breeds used to control the movement of other animals

hound group: breeds that search for hunted animals by smell and sight

littermates: a group of animals born at the same time

muzzle: the part of an animal's face that juts out and includes the jaw, mouth, and nose

non-sporting group: breeds of sturdy dogs that include a variety of types

prey: animals that are hunted and killed by other animals for food

purebred: an animal whose relatives are known and in whom the same traits have been passed down through generations

rabies: a disease that can cause death

shed: lose fur

sporting group: breeds noted for being active and alert; good in the water

toy group: breeds noted for their small size

tricolor: having three colors

vaccinations: injections of medicines that help prevent certain diseases

veterinary: medical treatment of animals

working group: breeds noted for their large size and strength

Index

Get the best
of both worlds.

AV2 bridges the gap between print and digital.

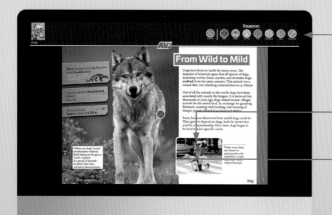

The expandable resources toolbar enables quick access to content including **videos**, **audio**, **activities**, **weblinks**, **slideshows**, **quizzes**, and **key words**.

Animated videos make static images come alive.

Resource icons on each page help readers to further **explore key concepts**.

Published by AV2
350 5th Avenue, 59th Floor
New York, NY 10118
Website: www.av2books.com

Library of Congress Cataloging-in-Publication Data

Names: Foran, Jill, author. | Gillespie, Katie, author.
Title: Dog / Jill Foran and Katie Gillespie.
Description: New York, NY : AV2 by Weigl, [2020] | Series: Pets we love | Includes index. | Audience: Grades 4-6 |
Identifiers: LCCN 2019048009 (print) | LCCN 2019048010 (ebook) | ISBN 9781791119164 (library binding) | ISBN 9781791119171 (paperback) | ISBN 9781791119188 (ebook other) | ISBN 9781791119195 (ebook other)
Subjects: LCSH: Dogs--Juvenile literature.
Classification: LCC SF427 .F634 2020 (print) | LCC SF427 (ebook) | DDC 636.7--dc23

LC record available at https://lccn.loc.gov/2019048009
LC ebook record available at https://lccn.loc.gov/2019048010

Printed in Guangzhou, China
1 2 3 4 5 6 7 8 9 0 24 23 22 21 20

022020
101319

Project Coordinator Sara Cucini
Art Director Terry Paulhus

Photo Credits
Every reasonable effort has been made to trace ownership and to obtain permission to reprint copyright material. The publishers would be pleased to have any errors or omissions brought to their attention so that they may be corrected in subsequent printings. AV2 acknowledges Alamy, Shutterstock, Minden, iStock, and Wikimedia Commons as its primary photo suppliers for this title. Image p. 26 courtesy of A.F. Archive.